THE LIFE AND WISDOM OF

MARGARET
OF SCOTLAND

THE 'SAINTS ALIVE' SERIES

THE LIFE AND WISDOM OF

MARGARET

OF SCOTLAND

E.C. Langdon

Written and Compiled by

LAVINIA BYRNE

ALBA·HOUSE · NEW·YORK

SOCIETY OF ST. PAUL, 2187 VICTORY BLVD., STATEN ISLAND, NEW YORK 10314

The Scripture quotations contained herein are from The New Revised
Standard Version of the Bible, Anglicized Edition, copyright © 1989,
1995 by the Division of Christian Education of the National Council of
the Churches of Christ in the United States of America, and are used by
permission. All rights reserved.

British Library Cataloguing in Publication Data:
A record for this book is available from the British Library.

ISBN 08189 08661

Typeset in Monotype Columbus by
Strathmore Publishing Services, London N7.

Printed and bound in Great Britain by
Mackays of Chatham PLC, Chatham, Kent.

Hodder and Stoughton Ltd,
A division of Hodder Headline PLC,
338 Euston Road, London NW1 3BH

CONTENTS

INTRODUCTION

———◆———

Who are the saints and why should we bother to know about their lives? We are inclined to think of them as heroic people who did extraordinary things, or as people who suffered a great deal and were somehow specially gifted or good. What we then forget is that, in general, saints are people like us. They struggled to know themselves better, to be more kind and loving, more self-accepting, less neurotic. They did not always succeed. They thought their attempts to live with integrity would make them closer to other people and to God. Often what they then discovered was that other people became harder to love and that God simply disappeared.

Yet they kept up the struggle. They believed that they were given one chance, that they had to live with a certain generosity, because this life is a preparation for the full glory of the next life. They then learnt that we are given many chances because all is grace, and the Christian life is a life of grace. So their schemes and plans for being holy were dismantled. All that was asked of them was a readiness to accept the gifts of God, including the final gift of heaven.

Saints come from every walk of life. They are men and women who share our concerns about money, power, politics, peace, energy, food, war, death, sex, love, privacy, the inner life, the outer life, harmony, balance. What makes them distinctive is that they looked beyond themselves to know how best to live and they discovered that God shared their concerns. If we read about them nowadays, we do so out of more than simple curiosity. Their lives are worth reading because we can learn from them. We look for more than a good example, though. The saints seem to know more than we do; they have access to a deeper level of wisdom than our own. They are gurus for our times. So when we read about them, we are quite right to seek an insight into the mind of God, who calls and inspires us all to the heroism of holiness, however we ourselves happen to live. Holiness is for all, not just the few; for a holy life is no more than a life lived in the presence of God.

In our materialistic and agnostic age, do the saints still matter? Have they any wisdom for us, or are they simply a pious irrelevance? Margaret of Scotland was a reconciler and a reformer, a scholar and an embroideress, a wife and a mother. In her, the line of the old Saxon kings of England was linked with the new dynasty of the Norman kings. We know about her because her biographer, Turgot, wrote a lyrical account of her life. But what is the importance of this life nowadays? Why should we care? Margaret of Scotland stands at a key point in British history and is pivotal to the unravelling of its meaning. In our own times, as we face transition, devolution and the emergence of a new nationalism, her story has a curious relevance. It is a story for our age.

PART ONE

---•---

The Story of Her Early Years

Hidden Treasure

PART ONE

Hidden treasure

A hidden treasure with a chequered history
In 1887 the librarian at a parish library in a small
English village called Brent Ely in Suffolk offered
a shabby brown book for sale. It was a medieval
octavo volume, which he sent to Sotheby's, the
auctioneers in London. The Bodleian Library in
Oxford bought it for six pounds. The book's title
was *The Four Gospels, a manuscript on vellum of the
fourteenth century, illuminated in gold and colours.*
When experts at the Bodleian examined the
book, they discovered that the writing dated from
the eleventh century. They had an exciting find
on their hands: inside the flyleaf there was a
twenty-three-line poem which gave away the
identity of its true owner. It told the story of the
book's narrow escape when in the hands of a servant of Margaret, the Saxon princess who became
Queen of Scotland and a canonised saint.

She had a book of the Gospels beautifully adorned with gold and precious stones, and ornamented with the figures of the four Evangelists painted and gilt. All the capital letters throughout the volume were *radiant with gold*. She had always felt a particular attachment for the book; more so than for any of the others which she usually read. It happened that as the person who carried it was once crossing a ford, he let the book, which had been carelessly folded in a wrapper, fall into the middle of the stream. Unconscious of what had occurred the man quietly continued his journey; but when he wished to produce the book, suddenly it dawned upon him that he had lost it. Long was it sought, but nowhere could be found. At last it was discovered lying open at the bottom of the river. Its leaves had been kept in constant movement, but the action of the water and little coverings of silk which protected the letters of gold from becoming injured by contact with the leaves, were swept away by force of the current. Who could have imaged that the book was worth anything after such an accident as this?

Who could have believed that so much as a single letter would have been visible? Yet of a truth, it was taken up from the middle of the river so perfect, so uninjured, so free from damage that it looked as if it had not been touched by the water. The whiteness of the leaves and the form of the letters throughout the volume continued exactly as they had been before it had fallen into the stream, except that on the margin of the leaves towards the edge, the least possible mark of water might be detected. The book was conveyed to the Queen, and the miracle was reported to her at the same time; and she, having thanked Christ, valued it more highly than she had done before. Whatever others may think, I for my part believe that this wonder was worked by our Lord out of his love for this venerable Queen.

The narrator is a medieval priest, a man called Turgot. He was the Scottish Queen's loyal and devoted biographer. He wrote of the qualities he admired in Margaret: her justice, piety, mercy and love, but, above all, he had an eye for detail.

So he noticed the 'radiant' quality of the gold used in the Gospel book, a shade which is different from the burnished gold of twelfth-century work and which served – along with the faint marks of water – as evidence of the book's chequered history.

A Saxon princess

Margaret's own history was chequered too. To explore it is to become a sleuth, poking about in the remains of eleventh-century history, searching out the real characters behind the familiar parodies of *1066 and All That*, with its pastiche of the early medieval period. This is a drama with real players, a kind of animated Bayeux tapestry, where the women in their willowy hats and the men in their chain-mail turn towards us from the past and remind us of a harrowing story. They stand at a crossroads, symbols of what happened when the Saxons met the Normans and an unpromising past appeared poised to become an elegant future.

So who are the players in this dramatic story? First, we have Margaret herself. Her name means 'pearl' and Turgot made a great play on this, assuring us that we would discover a 'pearl of great price' if we undertook to learn about her. Then there is her sister Christian, or Christina, and her brother Edgar, who was to be briefly the uncrowned King of England. Margaret was the eldest of the three children and was born in 1045. Her father was Edward Atheling, her grandfather was Edmund Ironside, her great-grandfather was Ethelred the Unready: Saxon kings to a man. Yet Ethelred made a treaty with the Norman Duke Richard, an alliance which he sealed by marrying Richard's sister, Emma. The marriage set up an impossible situation for the future, because it became inevitable that a Norman should lay claim to the English throne.

This was not the only threat to the crown. In 1013, another enemy had appeared on the scene. This time the threat came from the north. Canute, the son of Sweyn I 'Forkbeard', King of the Danes, invaded and conquered the country. The following year, on the death of his father, his Danish warriors proclaimed him King of England. However, the *witenagemot* or *witan*, which gave counsel to the Anglo-Saxon kings, reinstated Margaret's great-grandfather, Ethelred, and Canute fled. The illusion of safety could not be sustained, however; peace was not yet possible. Canute returned in 1015 and soon had all of England under his control, apart from London.

When Ethelred died in 1016, the people of London chose his son, a Saxon prince, and crowned him king, calling him Edmund II (Margaret's grandfather). But then a new war broke out against the Danish enemy. Canute defeated the Saxons in battle at Ashingdon, Essex, in October 1016. The following month Edmund died and Canute became the undisputed king. He wanted peace with the Saxons and peace with his continental neighbours, so he married King Ethelred's widow, Emma of Normandy. This was good news for the kingdom but bad news for Margaret's family. In the event, Canute ruled as undisputed King of England and then his two sons, Harold and Harthacanute, succeeded him. The rightful heirs to the crown, the children of Edward Atheling, became increasingly isolated so, for safety's sake, their father undertook to send them to the court of Stephen, the King of Hungary.

Exile in Hungary

The story of their exile begins with a sea journey as the children went off into exile with their mother, Agatha. The Hungarians had a reputation for hospitality, and lived up to it. The Hungarian court was still influenced by the saintly memory of King Stephen who had died in 1038 and been replaced by King Peter. At the Hungarian court, Margaret's family found a warm welcome, but also a degree of security and sophistication that was unfamiliar to them. The Saxons were a warring people: they had an impossible shoreline to defend from Viking, Danish or Norman invaders. Margaret and her family soon discovered that things were very different in land-locked Hungary. The court was ordered according to Christian standards. Stephen had been baptised as a young man of seventeen; at twenty he got married and settled down to a pious and scholarly life. He introduced the Latin tongue to the court and his nobility soon chose to speak that language, copying the king and living by his values. He practised prayer and good works, love for his neighbour and goodwill to the poor and needy. The Church would later canonise him as a saint.

Stephen enjoyed a privileged relationship with Pope Sylvester II and received his crown directly from him. Sylvester wrote:

As your highness did not disdain to undertake the apostolic office of proclaiming and spreading the faith of Christ we feel moved to confer benefits upon your excellency and this special privilege: we permit, desire and request that as you and your successors will be crowned with the crown we send you, the wearing of the cross may serve you and them as an apostolic token, even so that, according to the teachings of God's mercy, you and they may direct and order in our and our successor's place and stead, the present and future churches of your realm.

Stephen was held before the imagination of young Margaret as the model of a Christian prince. In place of the warrior heroes of the Saxon court, here was a man who cultivated the friendship of monks and scholars, a man who valued prayer and learning, a man who wanted to help the poor. Significantly, he had brought Benedictine monks into Hungary, founding a monastery at Cannoholma in 1007.

Margaret was at an impressionable age and took in everything she saw. The little girl looked up to the memory of her new patron and looked closely around at her new home as well. For not only did Stephen play the part of a saintly Christian prince for her, but her mother took on a new role too, by flourishing in this setting. Agatha was a niece of the Holy Roman Emperor, Henry III, and fitted well into court life. We are told that she was 'of stature somewhat above ordinary, so that in carriage everything appeared Majestick; but the Excellencies of her mind and the Candour of her Soul and the Holiness of her life made her incomparably more pleasant in the eyes of Edward Atheling than the greatness of her extraction'.

'Extraction' is a quaint word, but it serves as a useful reminder of how important women were in securing peace. As a girl child, Margaret was to become a player in this rich and complicated world of dynastic hopes and aspirations. Would she be a pawn, would bishops, knights and rooks somehow 'take' her, or would she live her own life and eventually become a queen by right? A later biographer would write that she 'obtained the honours alike of royalty and saintship; she became one of the brightest patterns of every virtue in her own time and she became the source through which the blood and rights of the Imperial House of Wessex have passed to the Angevin, Scottish and German sovereigns of England'. So how did this happen? How did young Margaret, playing and learning and growing up in a Hungarian court, fulfil this destiny? Her father, Edward Atheling, had joined his family in Hungary. The chance of any restoration of his fortunes looked remote. The sons of Canute – Harold and Harthacanute – ruled in England for seven years following their father's death in 1035, and then, when they died, a new king came to the throne, a saintly man whom we know as Edward the Confessor.

The exiles return

In 1042, Edward was brought back from exile in Normandy. He was the son of the marriage which King Ethelred had made with Emma, his Norman bride. This made him Margaret's great-uncle. At the court in Normandy where he was raised, Edward had also acquired sophisticated tastes. He liked horses and hunting, but basically he was a books man and preferred talking about religion more than anything else. There was another problem which made him somewhat suspect: not only did he like talking about religion but he preferred speaking French. He went so far as to introduce Norman friends at the English court – all this long before the Battle of Hastings and the Norman Conquest. Things continental became fashionable and Edward the Confessor was unashamedly a European man.

He was pleased to leave questions of state and governance to Earl Godwine, a good Saxon. To secure his friendship, Edward married Eadgyth, who was Godwine's daughter. Yet the marriage remained unconsummated, for Edward had vowed himself to a life of chastity. This presented fresh dynastic dilemmas. At the very moment at which the English people could have been forgiven for hoping for a little dynastic security, they ended up with a king who thought sanctity ruled out the fruits of marriage.

Nature abhors a vacuum, especially one created willingly by a childless king, and soon a new heir apparent emerged. Godwine's son, Harold, took to waiting in the wings, hoping that he could soon take over the kingdom. Not unnaturally, the *witan* panicked and sent for 'Edward the Exile', as Margaret's father, the Atheling, had come to be called. He was the dream candidate, the man who had not been exposed to Norman influences, a healthy Saxon with a son and heir – and two daughters. The children represented a wealth of opportunities, because they could be married off and so lock into new dynastic settlements which might secure the promise of a more certain future.

The little family set sail again. Margaret and

her brother and sister embarked on a fresh adventure, leaving the security of the Christian kingdom of Hungary and the saintly example of Stephen for something altogether more rough and uncertain. Is this the moment when Margaret's true Christian identity began to be forged? Hungary was fine. To be a princess in exile was to exude promise. What would happen in the rough and tumble of ordinary life, especially a life which appeared to offer much, but which, in the event, could not deliver?

In the place of hope, Edward's family was soon bereaved. They had come to England on the wings of a promise, but tragedy and death took over. In the words of one chronicler: 'Edward having received these News took journey with a fair train of Hungarian Lords and Gentlemen and arrived happily in London.' Edward the Atheling, the heir apparent, was forty-one years old when he arrived in England. Yet within a short period he had died and his family were once more cast upon the goodwill of others, in this case, Edward the Confessor and his courtiers. The date was 1057. What would happen to Agatha, Margaret and her sister Christina? What would be the fate of Margaret's little brother, Edgar, an inadequate and feeble lad who now became the focus of dynastic conflict?

In 1065, one of Edward the Confessor's dearest projects came to fruition. He wanted to build a religious memorial as a statement of his faith. There was already a church in east London dedicated to St Paul. He determined to build one in the west dedicated to St Peter so he chose a spot where his West Minster could be built. On the day when the new church was to be consecrated, the king was taken ill. He died on 5 January 1066 and was buried in the church he had just built. The year 1066 was to be a turning point for the kingdom. The Bayeux tapestry shows a comet at one point, a prescient image of conflict and change.

Who would Edward's successor be? There were two strong candidates, Harold, son of Earl Godwine, the Saxons' candidate, and William, the natural son of Duke Robert of Normandy. The true heir, Edgar, was out of the running, despite the wishes of some of the Saxon warriors.

Once again Margaret's family were at the centre of a storm. There is a curious irony about the fact that a bastard son of Robert of Normandy should emerge as a front runner. In the brave new world of the Norman Conquest, would the role of women somehow change? Would their value be displaced, or located in a new place?

Harold seized the throne, but within the year William of Normandy was crowned King of England at West Minster, on Christmas Day 1066. Margaret was now twenty-one. What would her future be? Who were her friends; who were her enemies? One important friend soon emerged: Lanfranc, a Benedictine monk from the monastery of Bec in Normandy, was consecrated Archbishop of Canterbury on 15 August 1070. A chronicler wrote: 'A number of bishops and abbots, with a great concourse of the clergy and people, were present at the ceremony. The inhabitants of the whole of England, whether present or absent, were raised to the highest pitch of joy, and would indeed have offered boundless thanks to God if they had known how much good Heaven was then bestowing on them.' Lanfranc was to be an important influence on Margaret: he was a reformer and would become her mentor and friend.

Exile in Scotland

Meanwhile, Margaret had fled the country once again, with her mother, brother and sister. Intending to return to Hungary, she was swept along the east coast of Britain and arrived in Scotland, landing in the Firth of Forth. At the royal fort of Dunfermline, the Scottish King, Malcolm, heard that relatives of Edward the Confessor had arrived there and went down to welcome them, attended, as his chronicler reported, 'by a gallant train of his nobility to receive them with great honour. He saluted Edgar and all his train with a cheerful countenance and conducted them to his palace with so much sweetness and goodness that they had reason from that happy minute to bury in oblivion all their former misfortunes.'

Malcolm was the son of Duncan, Macbeth's famous victim. He had to struggle to regain his throne, eventually slaying Macbeth in 1057. He had strengthened his hand by marrying Ingibiorg, the widow of Thorfinn, Earl of Orkney. When the twenty-one-year-old Margaret arrived in Scotland, Malcolm was newly widowed. Not surprisingly, the *Anglo-Saxon Chronicle* tells us that 'King Malcolm began to yearn for Edgar's sister as his wife'. England had little to give her; Hungary would have proved a dead end. Here in Scotland, something new was offered to her.

The early historians tell us, 'And this Edgar's sister Margaret, King Malcolm united to himself in wedlock with the consent of her kindred; a woman noble in her royal descent, but much more noble in her prudence and religion. And by her zeal and industry the king himself laid aside his barbarity of manner and became more honourable and more refined.' This is a discreet account of the situation. The truth of the matter is that Margaret was marrying an out-and-out barbarian. Malcolm could neither read nor write. His greatest enthusiasm was reserved for savage attacks on his English neighbours, and his court was neither particularly honourable nor refined.

The *Anglo-Saxon Chronicle* is more eloquent: 'She was to increase God's praise in the land and to direct the king from the erring path and to bend him to a better way, and his people with him; and to suppress the evil customs which the people had formerly used, even as afterwards she did.' Margaret's influence was to be twofold. She would reform the king – and with him his people. She would also reform the Church. Furthermore, a chronicler called Freeman noted:

> There was no need for Margaret to bring a new religion into Scotland, but she gave a new life to the religion she found existing there, and she made changes in various points where the traditions of the Scottish Church still differed from the received practice of Western Christendom … No royal marriage was ever more important in its results for both of the countries concerned. It was through Margaret that the old kingly blood of England passed into the veins of the descendants of the Conqueror; it was in her daughter, the heiress of her virtues, that the green tree began to return to its place.

Each of these sources suggests that Margaret the Christian reformer had three roles: her influence was to be exercised as wife, as queen and as mother. It is easy to be sentimental about these three threads or areas of influence, because each of these words carries a strong stereotype. What makes Margaret truly remarkable – and more than a plaster-cast saint – is the fact that she reinvented the roles and became a truly powerful and influential woman, as well as a saint.

Margaret's influence

What was Scotland actually like when Margaret arrived there? And, more particularly, what was it like in the court at Dunfermline? The name means 'the tower by the crooked stream'. We read in the *Douay Chronicle* that 'her palace, furniture, offices, maids of honour, table and all that appeared externally, were indeed suitable to the state and dignity of a Queen, but her secret life was such as became a true servant of God'. This picture is amplified by details from Turgot:

It was due to her that the merchants who came by land and sea from various countries brought with them for sale different kinds of precious wares which until then were unknown in Scotland. And it was at her instigation that the natives of Scotland purchased from these traders clothing of various colours, with ornaments to wear; so that from this period, through her suggestion, new costumes of different fashions were adopted, the elegance of which made the wearers appear like a race of new beings.

This immediately sounds like a benign and humanising influence. Margaret enjoyed colours and fabrics. She enjoyed decorating her home. She appears to have realised that such things would have a civilising effect on her husband and his court. The lie is given to those who wish to emphasise only her spiritual influence. She began with the fabric of her own house, realising that a Word who is made flesh has to be honoured in the body, in what we see and touch and love. In turn these give the context within which we practise any austerities or private disciplines of denial. Turgot again: 'She added to the state of the royal palace, so that not only was it brightened by the many coloured apparel worn in it, but the whole dwelling blazed with gold and silver; since the vessels employed for serving the food and drink to the king and the nobles of the realm were of gold and silver, or at least were gild and plated.'

Margaret made a home, and it was a comfortable and elegant one. If she fed the poor and knelt down at their feet and served them, it was because she wanted to do good, not demolish the structures which enabled her to have money, power and influence to exercise on their behalf. To read her story in any other way would be to impose late-twentieth-century ideas of equality on it. Turgot put it like this: 'By means of her temporal possession she earned for herself the rewards of heaven; for there, where her heart was, she had placed her treasure also. And since before all things she sought the kingdom of God and His justice, the bountiful grace of the Almighty freely added to her honours and riches in abundance.' The modern biographer does have a problem with interpreting Margaret, however. Not only are we tempted to read her story through our own eyes, but we also have none of her own written texts to go by. Margaret did not keep a journal or notes about her inner life. In this sense her authentic voice is missing, so everything we know about her is filtered to us through the pen of Turgot, who became Bishop of St Andrews.

He describes her first actions on becoming queen:

She had no sooner attained this eminent dignity than she built an eternal memorial of her name and devotion in the place where her nuptials had been held. The noble church which she erected there in honour of the Holy Trinity was to serve a threefold purpose; it was intended for the redemption of the king's soul, for the good of her own, and for securing to her children prosperity for this life and in that which is to come. This church she beautified with rich gifts of various kinds, amongst which, as is well known, were many vessels of pure and solid gold for the sacred service of the altar about which I can speak with greater certainty since, by the Queen's orders, I myself for a long time had all of them under my charge. She also placed there a cross of priceless value, bearing the figure of Our Saviour, which she had caused to be covered with the purest gold and silver and studded with gems, a token even to the present day of the earnestness of her faith.

The act of building this church tells us a great deal about the focus of Margaret's life. Scotland did have a rich religious past by the time she arrived there, yet it was a Celtic past and this made it suspect to Margaret and her new ally Lanfranc, the Archbishop of Canterbury. The fact that she added a chancel, apse and tower to a church which already stood at Dunfermline demonstrates her tact, however: she preferred to augment and enhance the existing spiritual life of the nation, rather than uproot the more primitive traditions which she found in place. As a reformer, Margaret was to be a woman of vision, but also one of immense diplomacy.

Is this how she brought Malcolm round so successfully? Turgot tells us:

He could not but perceive from her conduct that Christ dwelt within her; nay, more, he readily obeyed her wishes and prudent counsels in all things. What ever she refused, he refused also; whatever pleased her, he also loved for the love of her. Hence it was that, although he could not read, he would turn over and examine books which she used either for her devotions or her study; and whenever he heard her say that she was fonder of one of them than the others, this one he too used to look at with special affection, kissing it and often taking it in his hands. Sometimes he sent for a worker in precious metals, whom he commanded to ornament the volume with gold and gems, and when the work was finished, the King himself used to carry the volume to the Queen as a kind of proof of his devotion.

The King, too, learnt to enhance what he found, to add to its beauty by embellishment, and in so doing to serve Christ.

PART TWO

---◆---

The Wisdom of Margaret

New Ways

PART TWO

———————◆———————

New Ways

The church of the Culdees

The novelist Melvyn Bragg has written a very successful novel called *Credo*. It is set in seventh-century Ireland and Northumbria, and the high point of the book is the Church Synod of Whitby, which was held in the year 664. Whitby was the climax of a controversy which had raged between members of the Celtic Church and those of the Roman Church. They fought over different traditions and religious practices. When Pope Gregory sent Augustine as his missionary to Canterbury in the year 597, one of his tasks was to bring the Celts to order. Hardly the stuff of a rattling good novel – yet this is what *Credo* turns out to be. The story is peopled with saints and sinners, with characters as ambitious and as batty as in any other society – with real human beings, in fact.

When Margaret began her reforms of the

Church in Scotland, this was the historical back-drop with which she became concerned. She too came up against saints and sinners, people with entrenched views and customs, as well as zealous reformers. For hers is the eleventh-century contribution to the same ancient controversy. She was the equivalent of an Augustine in her own times: the outsider who came in initially as an observer and increasingly became an advocate for the triumph of the new ways over the old. The church extension which she built at Dunfermline was an addition to what was called a church of the Culdees. These were wandering hermits and clerics who kept the Celtic tradition alive and who exemplified both its strengths and its weaknesses.

Celtic spirituality

In our own times, 1997 saw the fourteen-hun-dredth anniversary of Augustine's arrival on the coast of Kent in southern England. The event was celebrated with a series of pilgrimages as people walked again in the footsteps of the saint. They took in the length and breadth of Britain, visiting a variety of Christian shrines. One of the most important of these is Iona, a small island off the west coast of Scotland. This is a remarkable place, a site where for centuries holy people have made their way to God. They continue to do so by coming to live as members of what is called the Iona Community, or as simple pilgrims. For years it was a centre of Celtic Christianity, having been founded by Columba in 556. Recently, Celtic spirituality has begun to re-emerge there. This is an ancient tradition which claims to have wisdom for our times. How are we to understand this wisdom? Do we take sides with Margaret and the reformers or, in the light of subsequent history, should we seek out and find that which was lost, and try to integrate its insights into mainstream spirituality?

This begs several other questions. What is the wisdom of Iona? What is the wisdom of the Celtic tradition? As the celebrations continue for Augustine and for the triumph of 'mainstream' Christianity, this is an ideal moment to ask what was lost when the life, work and scholarship of the Irish monks and the Culdees were destroyed.

Is an interest in Celtic spirituality naive or does it have something to offer us all?

The Celtic way of life

Celtic spirituality is interesting first of all as a way of life. It developed independently of the sources of the mainstream or 'orthodox' tradition. Ireland – where it originated – was never part of the Roman Empire, so the religious and domestic life of the Celtic people was not built up around cities, as in many European countries. Rather, the people lived in extended families, like tribes. They were ruled over by one of their own.

When Christianity first came to Ireland it adapted to local custom. Bishops and dioceses were an alien idea and fitted badly, for they seemed to be about the management of territories, rather than of communities of people. But monks and monasteries made total sense, as they built on community structures and did not cut across them. So Irish monasticism flourished and took hold of the people's imagination. They went on living as they had done, but some of their families were now families of monks. Their abbots were simple but wise leaders who took care of their own. Interestingly, some of the monks were not what we mean by monks at all. They were married people who happened to live and pray alongside those who chose the single life as a way of coming to God.

This was a very integrated way of living. No wonder that a very integrated spirituality would emerge from it: one which put great value on everyday things, on nature, on the weather, on growth and pattern and design. One which would seek and find God in all things, present in every moment and event, absent from none.

When Margaret dedicated the church at Dunfermline to the Blessed Trinity, she established a link with the very heart of the Celtic tradition. For no other mystery communicates quite so well the sense of Oneness and of variety which lies at the centre of this spiritual tradition, as this Celtic prayer shows:

> God makes the light of the sun to shine,
> He surrounds the moon and the stars,
> He has made wells in the arid earth,

Placed dry islands in the sea.
He has a Son co-eternal with himself,
And the Holy Spirit breathes in them;
Not separate are the Father and the Son
and the Holy Spirit.

Green martyrdom

So Celtic spirituality advocates an integrated way of living, but also a deeply adventurous one. The Celts invented the term 'green martyrdom'. What does that mean?

What drove St Columba away from Ireland to Scotland in his little wooden and leather circular boat, the traditional Celtic craft known as a coracle? Or St Columbanus to Gaul, as France was then called? Or the Irish abbot, Fursey, to East Anglia? Or Colman to Lindisfarne? And, supremely, what drove Brendan the Navigator on his astonishing journeys? St Brendan's little coracle has recently been re-created and intrepid sailors have repeated his journey, travelling to Scotland, Wales and Brittany, and even as far as Newfoundland, right across the Atlantic. The traveller in Margaret must surely have been attracted by this part of the tradition.

Why did the Irish abbots leave the security of home and set off on such extensive journeys, committing their lives to the rolling waves of the sea? Is there anything in what they did which can inspire or caution us? The logical answer is that they were driven by a desire to preach the word of God. They wanted to go to the ends of the known earth so that the gospel could be proclaimed. After all, the great words with which Matthew's Gospel ends are a challenge to any Christian: 'Go therefore and make disciples of all nations, baptising them in the name of the Father and of the Son and of the Holy Spirit, and teaching them to obey everything that I have commanded you. And remember, I am with you always, to the end of the age' (Matt. 28:19–20).

But the Celtic missionaries seem to have been driven by something even more radical than that passage from the Bible. They undertook an external journey – through time and space – because they knew from the depths of their being that they were also engaged on an interior journey. The perilous skidding across wild seas mirrored the journey towards God which they were conducting in the depths of their souls. 'Red martyrdom', the literal death which previous martyrs had endured for their faith, was no longer available. In its place came this 'green martyrdom', the journey away from home as a critical acknowledgment of the desire to be with God. In words from the Book of Genesis, we are reminded that Abraham too was called away from the familiar and the known to go on just such a journey.

> Now the Lord said, 'Go from your country and your kindred and your father's house to the land that I will show you. I will make of you a great nation, and I will bless you, and make your name great, so that you will be a blessing. I will bless those who bless you, and the one who curses you I will curse; and in you all the families of the earth shall be blessed' (Gen. 12:1–3).

This is heroism on a grand scale, a heroism which inspired great prayers. St Fursey, the man from Ireland who brought the faith of his people to East Anglia, wrote of what he discovered on his journey in this prayer. This is what the Celtic spiritual tradition offered Margaret:

> The arms of God be around my shoulders,
> the touch of the Holy Spirit upon my head,
> the sign of Christ's cross upon my forehead,
> the sound of the Holy Spirit in my ears,
> the fragrance of the Holy Spirit in my
> nostrils,
> the vision of heaven's company on my lips,
> the work of God's church in my hands,
> the service of God and the neighbour in
> my feet,
> a home for God in my heart,
> and to God, the Father of all, my
> entire being, Amen.

Celtic scholarship
The Book of Kells, a wonderful hand-painted and hand-written manuscript of the Gospels which is now in the library of Ireland's Trinity College in Dublin, is a Celtic masterpiece. The artists who created this early ninth-century text were monks, living in the tradition of their Celtic forebears,

inspired by the same sense of pattern and purpose and design. They made leather pages or vellum and paint and ink sing to the glory of God. They used colour and liquid gold to tell the most precious of all the narratives they knew: the story of the life, death and resurrection of Jesus as narrated in the four Gospels.

The front page of St John's Gospel shows John the evangelist, a bearded figure in a red cloak, sitting with a book on his lap. He looks out of the page at us, meeting the eyes of the scholar who created him, and meeting the eyes of the reader. When we turn the page, we know we will read the text which says, 'In the beginning was the Word': the prologue to John's Gospel. But for a moment we cannot bear to turn the page, because here, in these whirling Celtic images, we also see a representation of the Word, and the true scholar will read God from pictures as well as from a text.

That is the secret of Celtic scholarship. It takes note of what happens when the Word becomes flesh. It knows, for example, that being incarnate is desperately important. Disembodied, over-rarefied discussion separates and divides, whereas living in the flesh brings wholeness and the deepest sort of integrity. The beautiful circles and intricately patterned squares of the *Book of Kells* images are not simply there to decorate or to charm the eye. They make a theological statement; they say that there is order and pattern, that design, colour, harmony and balance are deeply important, and that if we gaze at them for long enough they will become part of us too. We will be swept into a world where mere words lose some of their grip on us and where our imaginations can fly.

These Irish and Scottish scholars were great learners. They painted pictures of flying fish and swimming birds, of dragons, monsters and every type of bird and beast. They tell stories of extra-ordinary narrative power and even greater imagination, for they tell it how it is, with the whole of themselves: will, memory, imagination, the breath they breathe, the gestures they make and the whole sweep of their hearts. Nothing is left out; all can be brought into work and love and art. For God is in all and all is in God.

That exuberance and energy was not entirely lost to the Christian community when missionaries from Rome descended on the Celtic Church and ran it into the ground at the Synod of Whitby. Roman and Celtic practices met in a headlong collision, however, and Rome apparently won. Among their disputes were different systems for calculating the date of Easter, for cutting the monks' hair and for running a model Christian community: a random list of things which nowadays may seem quaint, but which, up until that time, had enabled a whole generation of scholars to follow a different star.

A prayer from St Columba of Iona puts the Celtic instinct into words:

> Be thou a bright flame before me,
> be thou a bright star above me,
> be thou a smooth path below me,
> be thou a kindly shepherd behind me,
> today, tonight and forever.

When Margaret undertook to see through the reforming ideals established so much earlier at the Synod of Whitby, how could she do so without destroying the Celtic mind?

A seamless garment
The blind academic John Hull, Professor of Religious Education at the University of Birmingham, wrote a book called *Touching the Rock*. The rock in question was the altar at the Abbey church on the island of Iona, the great centre of Celtic spirituality founded by St Columba. For John Hull, the experience of touching that rock, which he relayed with a power and passion given quite specially to a blind man, was an experience of God. Today the Celtic magic still works for people who go to Iona and discover God in the material reality of the Abbey and the island.

But there is more to Celtic spirituality than that solid rock and the stability it represents. There is also the moving, dancing, spiritual life of a people who lived close to nature and were inspired in their quest for God by the cycle of life and death, of light and dark, and of the changing seasons. This Celtic prayer is for a woman as she milks her cow:

Give the milk, my treasure!
Give the milk, my treasure!
Give the milk and thou'lt have the blessing
  of the King of the earth,
The King of the sea,
The King of heaven,
The King of the angels,
My treasure!

This is a prayer from a seamless world, one where heaven and earth talk to each other through the familiar routine of human living, and the veil between them is thin. God is there in the activities of everyday life: the washing, the cleaning and the child-rearing; the preparation of the soil, the sowing of crops and their harvesting; hauling a sail and making your way out to sea for a catch of fish. These normal activities secure access to the divine presence, rather than taking us away from the King of the earth, sea, heaven and angels.

This is an insight which we badly need at the moment, because much contemporary interest in nature sentimentalises it. For Celtic farmers and fishermen, nature was not a friendly environment or even an environment to be befriended. It was where they lived and what gave them their food. They would be baffled by some of the concerns voiced by present city-dwellers about the state of the countryside, or by the desire we have to save time and take shortcuts in our production of food. They had no choice but to go with the rhythms of light and dark and the seasons. They lived within nature, within created reality.

That is why they could pray from within it and live comfortably with the idea that God was close to them and concerned about what interested them. God would be there with all the stability of the rock altar in the Abbey at Iona, and living and dying were part of the ultimate journey: the journey through monastic-style living as part of a great family of faith; the journey through a world of scholarship where the heart, mind and imagination could work together; the journey to the final place of rest – the rock we can all touch. This sense of blessing inspires another Celtic prayer:

On your heads and your houses the blessing
   of God
in your coming and going the peace of God
in your life and believing the love of God
at your end a new beginning
   the arms of God to welcome you and bring
   you home.

Margaret's reforms

This was the world, then, which Margaret met
when she undertook to help reform the Church
in Scotland. Under a less generous and less gra-
cious hand than hers, the casualties would have
been far greater, for Roman order and discipline
were diametrically opposed to the 'extremes'of
the Culdee tradition. Yet she grasped the nettle,
and at St Andrews in 1074 she convoked a meeting, or council, of church leaders. There were five
areas in particular which attracted her attention.
The first was to do with the observance of a fast
during Lent. The Scottish tradition had been to
undertake a thirty-six-day fast to prepare for the
feast of Easter. Elsewhere in Europe a forty-day
fast was observed. The number of days had some

significance in the wider world: it was about conformity to a norm which was observed elsewhere in the great Christian Church of the West.

Her next reform carried the same force. Traditionally the Culdees did not receive Communion or the Sacrament of the Lord's Supper. Their sense of unworthiness made them reluctant communicants, especially at Easter-time. But Margaret believed that Easter should be celebrated by going to Communion. Indeed, she thought that their kind of abstinence took something away from the true celebration of the feast day. In the *Douay Chronicle* we read that Margaret told the faithful – and their priests:

> Do not therefore excuse your negligence with the pretence of unworthiness, but be careful of the preparation with which you ought to come unto this Feast. Examine the state of your souls without flattery, connive at nothing, but after an exact scrutiny of your defects, eat of that bread and drink of that cup and you shall not find the rigour of the judgement of God.

The chronicler then adds: 'This discourse, fortified and quickened by the zeal of our holy Princess, convinced many of her subjects and brought them to communicate not only at Easter but also at the other feasts of the year.'

Scottish versions of the liturgy also came in for reform, as Margaret insisted on the observance of common practice and a standardised version of the Church's rituals. Traditionally, for example, the Culdees had not knelt down but had stood upright for all their prayers on the Lord's Day, as a sign of respect. Margaret's reforms changed this with the introduction of European customs, as well as the use of Latin throughout the liturgy. This could look like the imposition of foreign cultural norms and, at the time, it must have felt like that as well. The truth is more complicated, however, for somehow Margaret understood that ritual serves a pastoral purpose as well as liturgical one, and she wanted to communicate this. To provide the faithful with a reliable set of words and gestures is to introduce security and safety into their lives. It takes the worship and praise of God to a new place, one which is not influenced by the feelings or talents of the president or celebrant, but one which respects the faithful presence and observance of the people of God. Ultimately it focuses attention on God, rather than the servants of God.

It was the same with the custom of keeping the Sabbath. This had fallen out of practice in certain Scottish circles and Margaret was concerned to restore due reverence for it. In some Culdee churches, controversy had also arisen about the actual day of the Sabbath. Was it Saturday, the day when God rested after making his creation? Or was it Sunday, the first day of the new week, the day on which Jesus rose from the dead? Margaret made provision for Sunday to be observed as the Sabbath and for it to held in high esteem. She quoted Pope Gregory, saying, 'We must cease from earthly labour upon the Lord's day and we must devote ourselves entirely to prayer, so that upon the day of the Lord's Resurrection we may make expiation for such negligences as we may have committed during the six days.'

Her last reform was to do with marriage. The custom had arisen in the Irish church that a man should marry his deceased brother's wife, or his stepmother if his father died. This had become common practice in Scotland too. Margaret resisted it and declared such marriages unlawful. Her energy and sense of authority were astonishing, for she pushed these reforms through by sheer force of logic and the strength of her scholarship. Turgot comments: 'For everything she proposed she supported so strongly by the testimonies of the Sacred Scriptures and the teaching of the Holy Fathers, that no one on the opposite side could say one word against them; nay, rather, giving up their obstinacy and yielding to reason, they willingly consented to adopt all she recommended.'

Margaret's children

How Margaret found time to give birth to and raise eight children, when so much of her energy was directed towards Church reform, was taken as proof of her sanctity by her biographers. We gain an insight into her role as mother and nurturer not from an account of her relationships with her own children, however, but rather from Turgot's chapter on her observance of Lent.

> When it was morning she rose from bed and devoted a considerable time to prayer and the reading of the Psalms, and while thus engaged, she performed the following work of mercy. She ordered that nine little orphans utterly destitute should be brought in to her at the first hour of the day, and that some soft food such as children at that tender age like, should daily be prepared for them. When the little ones were carried to her she did not think it beneath her to take them upon her knee, and to get their pap ready for them, and this she put into their mouths with the spoon which she herself used.

Her notion of family and family life was inspired by her reading of the Rule of St Benedict. She saw the family as an organic whole, where everyone had their own place and entitlements and where they could safely grow and develop in the knowledge and love of God.

She had six sons and two daughters. Between them the sons secured two hundred years of peace for Scotland, by providing an unbroken line of seven kings. The two daughters, Matilda and Mary, married King Henry I of England and Eustace, the Count of Boulogne, respectively. It was for Matilda that Turgot wrote his account of Margaret's life. When Margaret died, her death tunic was preserved at Dunfermline and was subsequently used by queens of Scotland when they were giving birth to their children. It was reckoned to bring comfort and consolation, as well as good fortune.

Her death

In the spring of 1093, aged forty-eight, Margaret fell ill. On 13 November that year, having been confined to bed for six months, her condition became dramatically worse. Malcolm was away on another military expedition, or so she thought. In fact he was dead, slain along with their eldest son, Edward. One of the other boys, Edgar, announced the news to his mother as she lay dying. She went to God with the words,

'Grant me freedom', on her lips. The priest who watched her die wrote: 'Her departure was so calm, so tranquil, that we conclude her soul passed to the land of eternal rest and peace.' Such was the verdict of an age of faith on a woman of great faith and natural piety, a woman of great intelligence, diplomacy and tact, a reformer and a powerful agent of change. She was canonised on 19 June 1250.

PART THREE

Turgot's Life of Margaret of Scotland

Written for her daughter Matilda, Queen of England

A shortened version

PART THREE

Turgot's Life of Margaret of Scotland

The Prologue

O the honourable and excellent Matilda, queen
of the English, Turgot, servant of the servants of
St Cuthbert, sends the blessing of peace and
health in this present life, and in that which is to
come the chief good of all good things.

You have, by the request you made, commanded me that I should narrate for you the par-
ticulars of the life of your mother, whose
memory is held in veneration. These your com-
mands and wishes I willingly obey; nay, more, I
venerate them exceedingly, and I respectfully
congratulate you – whom the King of the Angels
has raised to the rank of Queen of England –
that you desire not only to hear about the life of
your mother, who ever yearned after the
Kingdom of the Angels, but further, to have it
continually before your eyes in writing, that so,
although you were but little familiar with her

face, you might at least have a perfect acquaintance with her virtues.

Chapter I
St Margaret's noble descent. Her virtues as a queen and as a mother.

Many, as we read, have got their name from a quality of their mind, so that in their regard there is shown a correspondence between the word forming their name and the grace they have received. The same thing was true of this virtuous woman. She was called Margaret, and in the sight of God she showed herself to be a pearl, precious in faith and works. She was indeed a pearl to you, to me, to all of us, yea, to Christ Himself, and being Christ's she is all the more ours now that she has left us, having been taken to the Lord.

Whilst Margaret was yet in the flower of youth, she began to lead a very strict life, to love God above all things, to employ herself in the study of the Divine writings, and therein with joy to exercise her mind. Her understanding was keen to comprehend any matter, whatever it might be; to this was joined a great tenacity of memory, enabling her to store it up, along with a graceful flow of language to express it.

While thus she was meditating upon the law of the Lord day and night, and, like another Mary sitting at His feet, delighted to hear His word, rather in obedience to the will of her friends than to her own, yea by the appointment of God, she was married to Malcolm, son of King Duncan, the most powerful king of the Scots. But although she was compelled to do as the world does, she thought it beneath her dignity to fix her affection upon the things of the world, and thus good works delighted her more than riches. This prudent queen directed all such things as it was fitting for her to regulate; the laws of the realm were administered by her counsel; by her care the influence of religion was extended, and the people rejoiced in the prosperity of their affairs. Nothing was firmer than her fidelity, steadier than her favour, or juster than her decisions; nothing was more enduring than her patience, graver than her advice, or more pleasant than her conversation.

She had no sooner attained this eminent dignity, than she built an eternal memorial of her name and devotion in the place where her nuptials had been held. The noble church which she erected there in honour of the Holy Trinity was to serve a threefold purpose; it was intended for the redemption of the king's soul, for the good of her own, and for securing to her children prosperity in the present life and in that which is to come. She left proofs of her devotion and fervour in various other churches, as witness the Church of St Andrews, in which is preserved a most beautiful crucifix erected by her there, and remaining even at the present day. Her chamber was never without such objects, those I mean which appertained to the dignity of the divine service. It was, so to speak, a workshop of sacred art: in which copes for the cantors, chasubles, stoles, altar-cloths, together with other priestly vestments and church ornaments of an admirable beauty, were always to be seen, either already made, or in course of preparation.

These works were entrusted to certain women of noble birth and approved gravity of manners, who were thought worthy of a part in the queen's service. No men were admitted among them, with the exception only of such as she permitted to enter along with herself when she paid the women an occasional visit. No giddy pertness was allowed in them, no light familiarity between them and men; for the queen united so much strictness with her sweetness of temper, so great pleasantness even with her severity, that all who waited upon her, men as well as women, loved her while they feared her, and in fearing loved her. Thus it came to pass that when she was present no one ventured to utter even one unseemly word, much less to do aught that was objectionable. There was a gravity in her very joy, and something stately in her anger. With her, mirth never expressed itself in fits of laughter, nor did displeasure kindle into fury. Sometimes she chided the faults of others – her own always – using that commendable severity tempered with justice which the Psalmist directs us unceasingly to employ, when he says, 'Be ye angry, and sin not.' Every action of her life was regulated by the balance of the nicest discretion, which impressed its own distinctive character upon each single virtue. When she spoke, her conversation was seasoned with the salt of wisdom; when she was silent, her silence was filled with good thoughts. So thoroughly did her outward bearing correspond with the staidness of her character that it seemed as if she had been from her very birth the pattern of a virtuous life. In fact, I may say, every word which she uttered, every act which she performed, shewed that she was meditating upon the things of heaven.

Nor was she less careful about her children than she was about herself. She took all heed that they should be well brought up, and especially that they should be trained in virtue. Knowing that it is written: 'He that spareth the rod hateth his son,' she charged the governor who had the care of the nursery to curb the children, to scold them, and to whip them whenever they were naughty, as frolicsome childhood will often be. Thanks to their mother's religious care, her children surpassed in good behaviour many who were their elders; they were always affectionate and peaceable among themselves, and everywhere the younger paid due respect to the elder. Thus it was that during the solemnities of the Mass, when they went up to make their offerings after their parents, never on any occasion did the younger venture to precede the elder; the custom being for the elder to go before those younger according to the order of their birth. She frequently called them to her, and carefully instructed them about Christ and the things of Christ, as far as their age would permit, and she admonished them to love Him always. 'O, my children,' said she, 'fear the Lord; for they who fear Him shall lack nothing, and if you love Him He will give you, my dear ones, prosperity in this life, and everlasting happiness with all the saints.' Such were this mother's wishes for her children, such her admonitions, such her prayers for them, poured out night and day with tears. She prayed that they might confess their Maker through the faith which works by love, that confessing they might worship Him, worshipping might love Him in all things and above all things, and loving might attain to the glory of the heavenly kingdom.

Chapter II
Her care for the honour of the realm and the discipline of the Church.

Nor need we wonder that the queen governed herself and her household wisely when we know that she acted always under the wisest of masters, the guidance of the Holy Scriptures. I myself have had frequent opportunities of admiring in her how, even amidst the distractions of lawsuits, amidst the countless cares of state, she devoted herself with wonderful assiduity to the study of the word of God, respecting which she used to ask profound questions from the learned men who were sitting near her. But just as no one among them possessed a deeper intellect than herself, so none had the power of clearer expression. Thus it very often happened that these doctors went from her wiser men by much than when they came. She sought with a religious earnestness for those sacred volumes, and oftentimes her affectionate familiarity with me moved me to exert myself to obtain them for her use. Not that in doing this she cared for her own salvation only; she desired that of others also.

First of all in regard to King Malcolm: by the help of God she made him most attentive to the works of justice, mercy, almsgiving, and other virtues. From her he learnt how to keep the vigils of the night in constant prayer; she instructed him by her exhortation and example how to pray to God with groanings from the heart and abundance of tears.

The queen on her side, herself a noble gem of royal race, much more ennobled the splendour of her husband's kingly magnificence, and contributed no little glory and grace to the entire nobility of the realm and their retainers. It was due to her that the merchants who came by land and sea from various countries brought along with them for sale different kinds of precious wares which until then were unknown in Scotland. And it was at her instigation that the natives of Scotland purchased from these traders clothing of various colours, with ornaments to wear; so that from this period, through her suggestion, new costumes of different fashions were adopted, the elegance of which made the wearers appear like a new race of beings. She also arranged that persons of a higher position should be appointed for the king's service, a large number of whom were to accompany him in state whenever he either walked or rode abroad. This body was brought to such discipline that, wherever they came, none of them was suffered to take anything from anyone, nor did they dare in any way to oppress or injure country people or the poor.

All this the queen did, not because the honours of the world delighted her, but because duty compelled her to discharge what the kingly dignity required. For even as she walked in state, robed in royal splendour, she, like another Esther, in her heart trod all these trappings under foot, and bade herself remember that beneath the gems and gold lay only dust and ashes.

Journeying thus onwards towards the heavenly country in thought and word and deed, this devout and god-worthy queen called on others to accompany her in the undefiled way, so that they with her might attain true happiness. When she saw wicked men she admonished them to be good, the good to become better, the better to strive to be best. Observing that many practices existed among the Scottish nation which were contrary to the rule of the right faith and the holy customs of the universal Church, she caused frequent councils to be held, in order that by some means or other she might, through the mercy of Christ, bring back into the way of truth those who had gone astray.

Among these councils the most important is that in which for three days she, with a very few of her friends, combated the defenders of a perverse custom with the sword of the Spirit, that is to say, with the word of God. It seemed as if a second Helena were there present, for as that queen in former days by citing passages from the Scriptures overcame the Jews, so in our times did Queen Margaret overcome those who were in error. In this discussion the king himself took part as an assessor and chief actor, being fully prepared both to say and do whatever she might direct in the matter at issue. And as he knew the English language quite as well as his own, he was in this council a very exact interpreter for either side.

Chapter III
Her piety. Her charity to the poor. Her redemption of
English captives. Her manner of passing Lent.

Thus it came to pass that this venerable Queen, who by God's help had been so desirous to cleanse His house from all filth and error, was found day by day worthier of becoming His temple, as the Holy Spirit shone ever brighter in her heart. And I know of a truth that she was such, because I not only saw the works which she did outwardly, but besides this, I knew her conscience, for to me she revealed it.

Let me speak first of all about her prayerfulness. In church no one was so silent and composed as she, no one so wrapt in prayer. Whilst she was in the house of God she would never speak of worldly matters, or do anything which savoured of the earth; she was there simply to pray, and in praying to pour forth her tears. Only her body was then here below, her spirit was near to God, for in the purity of her prayer she sought nothing but God and the things which are God's. As for her fasting, I will say this alone, that the strictness of her abstinence brought upon her a very severe infirmity.

To these two excellent gifts of prayer and abstinence she joined the gift of mercy. For what could be more compassionate than her heart? Who could be more gentle than she towards the necessitous? Not only would she have given to the poor all that she possessed; but if she could have done so she would have given her very self away. She was poorer than any of her paupers; for they even when they had nothing, wished to have something; while all her anxiety was to strip herself of what she had. When she went out of doors, either on foot or on horseback, crowds of poor people, orphans and widows flocked to her, as they would have done to a most loving mother, and none of them left her without being comforted. But when she had distributed all she had brought with her for the benefit of the needy, the rich who accompanied her, or her own attendants, used to hand to her their garments, or anything else they happened to have by them at the time, that she might give them to those who were in want; for she was anxious that none should go away in distress. Nor were her attendants at all offended, nay rather each strove who should first offer her what he had, since he knew for certain that she would pay it back two-fold. Now and then she helped herself to something or other out of the king's private property, it mattered not what it was, to give to a poor person; and this pious plundering the king always took pleasantly and in good part. It was his custom to offer certain coins of gold upon Maundy Thursday and at High Mass, some of which coins the queen often devoutly pillaged, and bestowed on the beggar who was petitioning her for help. Although the king was fully aware of the theft, he generally pretended to know nothing of it, and felt much amused by it. Now and then he caught the queen in the very act, with the money in her hand, and laughingly threatened that he would have her arrested, tried, and found guilty. Nor was it towards the poor of her own nation only that she exhibited the abundance of her cheerful and open-hearted charity, but those persons who came from almost every other nation, drawn by the report of her liberality, were the partakers of her bounty. Of a truth then this text may be applied to her, 'He hath dispersed abroad, he hath given to the poor, therefore his justice remaineth for ever.'

But who can tell the number of English of all ranks, carried captive from their own land by violence of war and reduced to slavery, whom she restored to liberty by paying their ransom? Spies were employed by her to go secretly through all the provinces of Scotland and ascertain what captives were oppressed with the most cruel bondage, and treated with the greatest inhumanity. When she had privately ascertained where these prisoners were detained, and by whom ill-treated, commiserating with them from the bottom of her heart, she took care to send them speedy help, paid their ransom and set them at liberty forthwith.

Since the church of St Andrews was much frequented by the devout, who flocked to it from all quarters, she erected dwellings on either shore of the sea which divides Lothian from Scotland, so that the poor people and the pilgrims might shelter there and rest themselves after the fatigues of their journey. She had arranged they should there find all that they needed for the refreshment of the body. Servants were appointed, whose especial duty it was to see that everything which might be required for these wayfarers should be always in readiness, and who were directed to attend upon them with all diligence. Moreover, she provided ships for the transport of these pilgrims both coming and going, nor was it lawful to demand any fee for the passage from those who were crossing.

During the season of Lent, it was the custom to bring three hundred poor people into the royal hall, and when they were seated round it in order, the king and queen entered; whereupon the doors were shut by the servants, for with the exception of the chaplains, certain religious and a few attendants, no one was permitted to be present at the giving of these alms. The king on the one side and the queen on the other waited upon Christ in the person of His poor, and served them with food and drink which had been prepared for this special purpose. When the meal was finished, the queen's wont was to go into the church, and there with long prayers, with tears and sighs to offer herself as a sacrifice to God. Upon holy days, in addition to the hours of the Holy Trinity, the Holy Cross, and Holy Mary, recited within the space of a day and a night she used to repeat the Psalter twice or thrice; and before the celebration of the Public Mass she caused five or six Masses to be sung privately in her presence.

These concluded it was time for the queen's repast. But before this was served she herself humbly waited upon twenty-four poor people whom she fed; for without reckoning the alms-deeds which I have already mentioned, throughout the course of the year she supported twenty-four poor as long as she lived. It was her will that wherever she lived they also should be living in the neighbourhood; wherever she went they were to accompany her. Not until after she had devoutly waited upon Christ in these His poor was it her habit to refresh her own feeble body.

Chapter IV
The Queen's preparation for her departure. Her sickness and happy death.

Summoning me to come to her privately, she began to recount to me in order the history of her life. When she had ended what she had to say about matters which were pressing, she then addressed herself to me, saying: 'I now bid you farewell. I shall not continue much longer in this world, but you will live after me for a considerable time. There are two things which I beg of you. One is, that as long as you survive you will remember me in your prayers; the other is, that you will take some care about my sons and daughters. Lavish your affection upon them; teach them before all things to love and fear God; never cease instructing them. When you see any one of them exalted to the height of an earthly dignity then, as at once his father and his master in the truest sense, go to him, warn him, lest through means of a passing honour he become puffed up with pride, or offend God by avarice, or through prosperity in this world neglect the blessedness of the life which is eternal.'

Shortly afterwards she was attacked by an infirmity of unusual severity, and was purified by the fire of a tedious sickness before the day on which God called her to Himself. On the fourth day preceding her death, while the king was absent upon expedition, and at so great a distance that it was impossible for any messenger, however swift, to bring her tidings of what was happening to him, she became sadder than usual. Then she said to me, for I was seated near her, 'Perhaps on this very day such a heavy calamity may befall the realm of Scotland as has not been for many ages past.' When I heard these words I paid no great attention to them, but a few days afterwards a messenger arrived who told us that the king was slain on the very day on which the queen had spoken the words narrated. As if foreseeing the future, she had been most urgent with him not to go with the army, but it came to pass – how I know not – that he failed to follow her advice. On the approach of the fourth day after the king's death, her weakness having somewhat abated, the queen went into her oratory to hear Mass; and there she took care to provide herself beforehand for her departure, which was now so near, with the holy viaticum of the Body and Blood of our Lord. After partaking of this health-giving food she returned to her bed, her former pains having assailed her with redoubled severity. The disease gained ground, and death was imminent. Her face was already covered with a deadly pallor, when she directed that I, and the other ministers of the sacred Altar along with me, should stand near her and commend her soul to Christ by our psalms. Moreover, she asked that a cross, called the Black Cross, which she always held in the greatest veneration, should be brought to her. There was some delay in opening the chest in which it was kept, during which the queen, sighing deeply, exclaimed, 'O unhappy that we are! O guilty that we are! Shall we not be permitted once more to look upon the Holy Cross!' When at last it was got out of the chest and brought to her, she received it with reverence, and did her best to embrace it and kiss it, and several times she signed herself with it. Although every part of her body was now growing cold, still as long as the warmth of life throbbed at her heart she continued steadfast in prayer. She repeated the whole of the Fiftieth Psalm, and placing the cross before her eyes, she held it there with both her hands.

Feeling now that death was close at hand, she at once began the prayer which is usually uttered by the priest before he receives the Body and Blood of our Lord, saying, 'Lord Jesus Christ, who according to the will of the Father, through the co-operation of the Holy Ghost, hast by Thy death given life to the world, deliver me.' As she was saying the words, 'Deliver me,' her soul was freed from the chains of the body, and departed to Christ, the author of true liberty; to Christ whom she had always loved, and by whom she was made a partaker of the happiness of the saints, as she had followed the example of their virtues. Her departure was so calm, so tranquil, that we may conclude her soul passed at once to the land of eternal rest and peace. It was remarkable that her face, which, when she was dying had exhibited the usual pallor of death, became afterwards suffused with fair and warm hues, so that it seemed as if she were not dead but sleeping. Her corpse was shrouded as became a queen, and was borne by us to the Church of the Holy Trinity, which she had built. There, as she herself had directed, we committed it to the grave, opposite the altar and the venerable sign of the Holy Cross which she had erected. And thus her body at length rests in that place in which, when alive, she used to humble herself with vigils, prayers, and tears.

FURTHER READING

FURTHER READING

Donaldson, Gordon, *Scotland: Church and Nation through 16 Centuries*, SCM Press, 1960

Menzies, Lucy, *Saint Margaret Queen of Scotland*, J. M. Dent and Sons Ltd, 1925

Raleigh, Sir Thomas, *Annals of the Church in Scotland*, Oxford University Press, 1921

Southern, R. W., *Western Society and the Church in the Middle Ages*, Penguin, 1970

Turgot, Bishop of St Andrews, *Life of St Margaret Queen of Scotland*, translated from the Latin by William Forbes-Leith SJ, Edinburgh, 1884

Saints for Young Christians

DAVID PREVITALI

Eighty-three fascinating stories relating the lives and experiences of nearly 100 saints are told here in an entertaining, catechetical fashion. Each emphasizes the way in which that particular saint lived the Good News of Jesus in his or her own life. The illustrations enhance the narrative and make it easier for the reader to identify and relate to the saint whose life and works are under discussion. Young people, parents and teachers alike will warm to the solid and yet devotional way in which this work makes the lives of the saints come alive.

Saints Gabriel Possenti, Passionist

GABRIEL CINGOLANI, C.P.

Falling in love is a fundamental event of life. It means not only getting the boy or the girl of one's dreams, but above all finding a reason for living life passionately. Francis Possenti of Assisi, who became Gabriel of Our Lady of Sorrows as a Passionist, fell in love with a girl, as was normal for an 18-year-old boy. But when he realized that there was also another way to fulfill himself in an overflowing of love: by spending his life for God and others. He gave himself so completely that at 24, his life had been used up. This is his story.

Thérèse of Lisieux and Marie of the Trinity

PIERRE DESCOUVEMONT

Marie-Louis Castel was 20 years old when she entered the Carmel of Lisieux in 1894 and became the novice of St. Thérèse of the Child Jesus. For the next 50 years she put into practice in her daily life the "little way" taught to her by her saintly novice mistress. Suffering terribly from a painful facial ulcer in the final years of her life, she remained always faithful to "the spirituality of the smile." Her favorite saying which she had learned from St. Thérèse and which she was known often to repeat was, "No! Life is not sad!" It's an attitude and outlook on life that is found on every page of this inspiring work.